PYROGRAPHY

-A WOODBURNING ART WORKBOOK

A Complete Step-by-Step Guide for Beginners, With Techniques, Tips and Tricks for Professional Enhancement in the Art

BY

Johnson Smith

Copyright © 2021 Johnson Smith

TABLE OF CONTENTS

CHAPTER ONE

THE BASIC CONCEPT OF PYROGRAPHY

The word "pyrography" basically means to write with fire. Pyrography is often referred to as "Woodburning". Pyrography can be applied to any recording surface (including wood, leather, paper, and gourds). We will consider those under Pyrography Mediums.

Additionally, pyrography may be regarded as the art of engraving patterns into a wood or other materials by the controlled application

of a heated tool developed for that purpose. Pyrography can be used to add decorative items to many wooden or leather items such as dishes, handbags, spoons, plates, bowls, etc.

PYROGRAPHY MEDIUMS

WOOD: The best wood for pyrography is softwood with close-knit patterns. This includes linden and pine, but maple and plywood also make for a great starting point. Always brush the surface before starting a smooth burn.

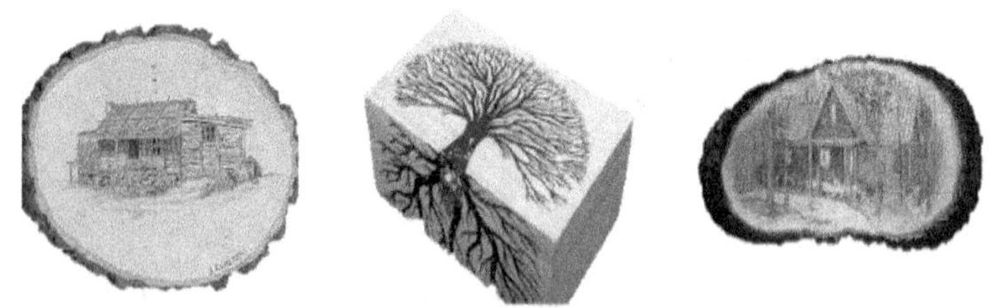

Pyrography on wood

LEATHER (ANIMAL SKIN): The skin burns at a lower temperature and its smooth surface is generally very easy to work with.

Finished products blackened vegetable belts, wallets, etc., are available now at most craft stores including bookmark bracelets.

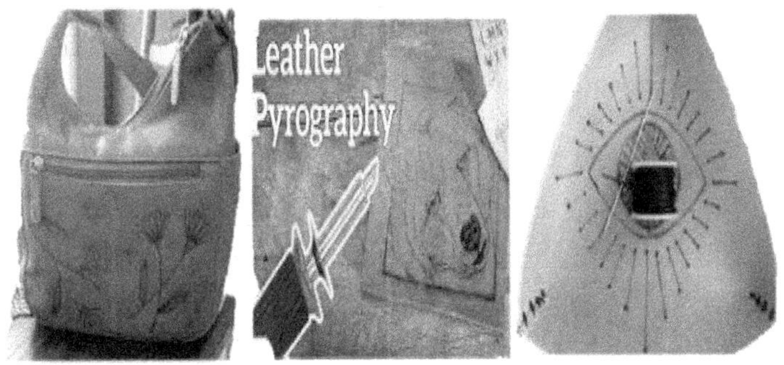

Leather pyrography

PAPER: Watercolor paper is the most popular for pyrography because of its heavy weight. Cold or hot-pressed paper and heavyweight will give the best results. 140-pound blocks work well and will keep the paper from melting under the heat of the writing instrument.

Pyrography on paper

GOURD: Sliced, cleaned, and dried hard-shell gourds are ideal for pyrography because they have a hard and porous, smooth, and slightly burnt surface.

Gourd pyrography

Reminder: Don't forget to burn with Personal Protective Equipment (PPE) like eye protection, nose mask, and hand gloves and in a well-ventilated area to prevent inhalation of toxic fumes from materials.

CHAPTER TWO

GATHERING MATERIALS

Only a few supplies are needed and most are available in a nice kit for beginners! In general, the two basic things that are required are wood and a pen (writing instrument) so that you can draw patterns on the surface.

No matter what you burn, you will always need a wood-burning tool. It doesn't have to be expensive either - you can burn it with a cheap wood-burning device as well as a professional combustion system.

There are some basic tools that you will need before you start burning wood. In general, as a beginner, you can purchase the basics. As you get stronger, you can add to your equipment as needed.

The Pyrography kit is available at your local craft store or online. For starters, this is a great way to get started with one of these wood toolkits.

The basic tools and supplies you will need are:

- Wood, leather, paper, or gourd
- Pen for burning
- Sandpaper, Graphite paper
- Eraser, adhesive tape, artist tape or painter tape, and ruler
- Mineral or Olive Oil (for the finishing)

Traditional pyrography can be done with any heated metal instrument. There are modern pyrography machines that can be divided into three main categories.

Fixed Point Burner: Fixed points resemble soldering irons in appearance. They are comprised of solid brass that is heated by an electronic element and operates at a steady temperature.

Cable Burner: These have temperature controls that are changeable. The writing tip is preheated by an electrical current passed across it directly. Some models have adjustable nibs that give rise to different effects.

Laser Cutter: These can be set up to burn material instead of cutting it entirely. Many laser cutters offer software setups for importing image files and transferring them to the board. Some laser systems are sensitive enough to burn on thin cards or even paper.

WOOD-TYPE SELECTION

Woods differ in their hardness, grain, shape, texture, color, and other natural properties.

Hardwoods: All woods can be classified as hard or soft. Coniferous or softwoods usually come from conifers. You may be familiar with some resin liquid and also a mild scent when burning on softwood.

Hardwood is made from deciduous trees. These hardwood trees can be divided into two different growing seasons each year: hot and cold season or rainy and dry season.

Wood is the dominant medium used

Earlywood: This type is often lighter in weight and color and relatively robust.

Latewood: It is often thicker, darker, and somewhat louder. Softwoods burn more rapidly than hardwoods. Hardwoods do not need a very high temperature to burn.

Grain: Granules are the orientation of xylocytes' fibrous constituents. It is crucial to sand-fine thoroughly before use for more effectiveness. If you stop applying pressure and the grain burns more slowly, the grain cannot deviate from the intended path with a wooden pen. Therefore, it is recommended that you burn more slowly with a focused direction on granular wood for achieving the desired objective.

The grain, when retained, gives the art

Shape: This is the natural pattern seen on the surface of the woodcut. When developing your wood, you should constantly consider the wood's natural appearance.

Texture: This refers to the texture on its surface that is rough or fine, even or rough to the touch.

Woodburning novices should avoid utilizing delicate or detailed designs on rough, thick wood. Conifers or softwoods tend to be fine or moderately coarse. With some textures, this may mean having to make up for it by going slower, or faster with a lighter touch on the toughest summer tree.

Color: It should be used primarily to enhance the natural beauty of a wood project. So don't always hide a beautiful figure, grain, shine, or color if available.

SIMPLE WOOD TOOLS

Walnut Hollow: It is thicker than the burning pens used in a professional burning system and should be further away from burning. This makes it a little more bizarre to use, but like any tool, the harder you work with it, the easier it gets.

Walnut Hollow Wood Burner

This particular walnut hollow tool does not have an adjustable temperature display, which means it heats up very quickly and then gradually cools down.

The trick is in knowing when the heat build-up starts so you can quickly lift the tool off the surface or work on the design a little faster. If you're not careful it can even make a hole in your piece. You always have different torch tips that you can use to create different lines and marks on your surface. You can also purchase a variety of burn tips, which are sold separately.

It can be frustrating to take the time to change the hints as this tool gets too hot and won't cool down too quickly. To speed up the work, you can remove the hot tip with needle-nose pliers and screw in a new tip.

PROFESSIONAL COMBUSTION SYSTEMS

There are many different brands of professional wood-burning systems on the market. In addition to the Walnut Hollow pens, you can also use the Nibsburner Blue Ribbon system.

Nibsburner Models

SAFE USE AND CARE OF YOUR TOOLS

Read all of the instructions that came with your tool. Make sure that the wood burner is disconnected and cooled. Screw the end you want into the wood burner. Plugin the wooden tool and let it heat up for at least 5 minutes. Carefully place the edge on the surface of the wood to burn into your design. Keep the pressure constant to burn evenly colored lines. Avoid applying excessive pressure to create darker lines as it can damage the nose.

Instead, keep the nose in the same spot until the burn creates the shade you want. When you finish the drawing in a line or shape, be sure to lift the wood-burning tool out of the wood. Leaving it on the wood surface can cause burns. If you want to change the nozzles, make sure the wood stove is not plugged in. and let it cool before touching the edge. Keep the noses in a sealed box to prevent damage. Alternatively, you can use needle pliers for removing hot noses. Be sure to lightly sand the end of the woodstove with gloves on. Use a soft cloth to clean your nose. This is done so that scraps of wood do not stay on the nose and become blunt.

WOOD ART FINISHING

Once you've burned your design onto the wood, you can use sandpaper to smooth out some rough spots. A soft cloth can also be used to wipe scraps of wood off the artwork.

Mineral oil or olive oil can be used to give the wood a nice shine. If you want a lacquered wood look, Lacquer or shellac can also be used.

BEST TOOLS FOR PYROGRAPHY

The Razertip Dual Burner is the greatest wood-burning equipment on the market for artists who take pyrography seriously due to its versatility and ability to manufacture intricate pieces. When you enter the world of pyrography, an excellent wood-burning tool for beginners is the Walnut Hollow Versa Tool because it is affordable. It offers variable temperature control and a range of accessories to get you started.

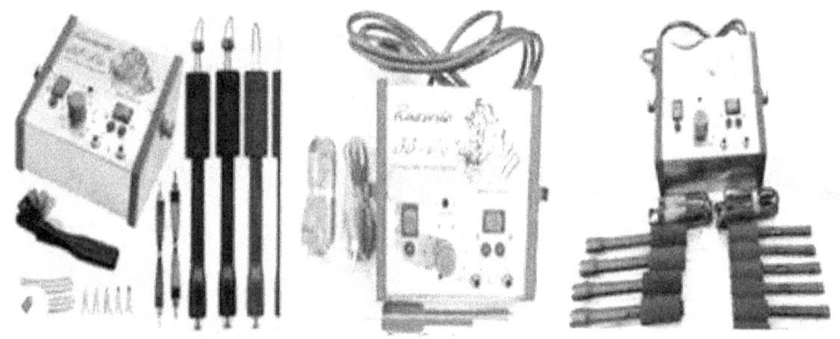

Razertip Dual Burner for Professional Pyrographers

PYROGRAPHY TOOLS STYLE

Copper often has a thicker edge, a larger hand, and longer heating and cooling periods (approximately five to eight minutes). Not suitable very for detailed work. These are better for general purposes like larger designs or signs as well as filling larger areas. Some have a double heat shield in order to keep your hand protected from the heat emanating from the pen tip.

PYROGRAPHY TOOLS WITH TEMPERATURE CHANGE

- Electronic temperature control
- Shorter heating and cooling intervals, up to a minute or two
- Smaller handles make it simpler to "save" or "draw" with these tools, faster heating for quicker design abilities
- Premium pencil points for finer work

Some have a dual pen feature that offers flexibility

FACTORS AFFECTING TOOL PERFORMANCE IN PYROGRAPHY

Several variables influence the effectiveness of a specific brand of pen. Based on how you intend to employ your pyrography instruments, you will choose which among these performance characteristics is most essential.

You may need a wood-burning tool that has details on how to optimize your wood carvings. Others may need some tips to help achieve different skin burn project designs. For the containers that you will be using the burn tools on, use this guide to learn what to look for.

When you are in the Pyrography Toolkit market, you have many factors to put into consideration. They include the following:

POWER

In general, many professional wood-tool makers tell you the more power the better. On paper, this is because the hotter the tip of your pyrography device, the faster you can print. However, excessive force will often result in early failure of the components of the combustion tool. It can also result in an undesirable tanned look (unless you want it to be).

The power is usually displayed in watts (x-volt amplifier). If you're looking for a quick branding tool, therefore, consider one that is not just more powerful overall but also has more amps. Additionally, think about the trend. Three-volt systems usually have heavier test leads. This means less detail in your signs. Two-volt systems generally offer thinner test leads. It would be perfect for additional in-depth research. Three-volt systems are usually found in artisanal wood burners. Two-volt systems are typically connected to variable-temperature burners.

TYPES OF TIPS AND STYLES

Your pyrography tool's tip makes an impression. Hence, you must get the right advice for your needs. Check out the tips below:

Interchangeable: Likely one of the most important features of detailed art, alternate tips will give you the flexibility required to produce detailed work. You can also work with fewer pyrography tools or wooden pens for changing the tips.

Unglazed: These tips are somewhat more robust and have a greater propensity to attract substances. The outcome is a simpler appearance with fewer errors. These are often used in pyrography and are suitable for huge, dark surfaces.

Polished: Such tips are indeed very smooth and enable for precise movement over surfaces. They give much more information and are often seen on variable-temperature burners.

Fixed: Solid edges heat up faster for a faster and smoother design.

HELPFUL ASSESSMENTS FOR PURCHASING TOOLS

When looking for craft materials and tools, it's not just performance to consider. For some, price and convenience are more important than anything else.

COMFORT

It is crucial that your pyrography instrument be comfortable to handle and operate, particularly if you want to use it often. Experience has revealed that craft instruments often have bigger handles that allow for continuous usage without cramping.

The handles of variable-temperature tools are often smaller, simpler to make, and less tiring to use for extended periods.

COSTS

The cost of wood-burning tools varies significantly. If you are just starting with art pyrography, you would do well starting with inexpensive models. While they may not be reliable or feature-rich in over time, they are a good place to start.

If you are professionally inclined to use a pyrography tool, modern innovative tools seem more expensive. However, it does offer better options and a good investment. These machines give you additional tips, all the power you need in detailed characters, and make for durability.

This is one of the greatest wood pyrography tools on the market, and it's apparent that many pros utilize the Razertip Dual Burner, that has a 10-amp output on hardwood tips, to further their craft. The outcome is an amazing fast pick-up time that allows you to plan faster and smoother. This is great for working seamlessly and leveraging your creative flow.

In addition, it contains variable temperature settings that let you adjust the heat density from "1" to "10". It is also engineered to limit waste so that you don't accidentally burn the wood you're working on, at even high heat. In addition to the more than 800 pen and edge combinations offered by Razertip, a variety of additional items are now available. It is one of the most flexible pyrography tools available on the market.

This wood engraving is designed for safety and reliability. It has a fixed circuit to ensure reliability marks every time you apply the pen. The Razertip unit can use other brands of pens. This is for users who prefer other items. The pen tips also heat up very quickly, so you don't have to wait.

The Razertip Dual Burner is recommended for high-level professionals who need incredible precision while burning. If you can't find Razertip in stock, Colwood Super Pro II is another great choice.

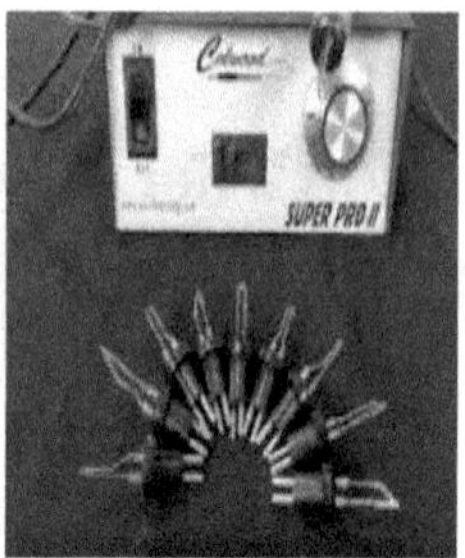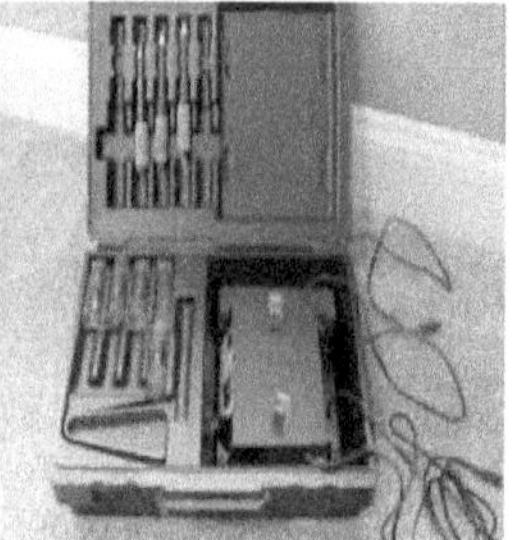

Colwood Super Pro II designed for high-level professional pyrography

It is among the finest pyrography and professional woodburning instruments available. It has several suggestions. It is an excellent option for those who like to invest in their work. It has a 60-watt wood burner with rapid heat response, allowing for fast and seamless design options. Due to digital voltage control, it is also possible to accurately alter the temperature. This function enables you to customize the edge's heat output to meet the specific needs of each job.

Additionally, the TRUArt Stage 2 Professional Wood Burner Detailer is exceptionally compact and lightweight. Consequently, it is exceedingly handy and allows users to create extremely exact annotations. Perfect for the most intricate masters. This pyrography toolkit has an additional 20 stunning tips!

If you are looking for a qualified and reliable pyrography detail specially made for various combustion environments such as wood, you can create incredibly detailed works of art with this leather, gourd, and paper kit. This wood engraving is designed for reliability and safety. It has a fixed circuit to ensure reliability marks every time you apply the pen.

The variable temperature settings on the Walnut Hollow Creative Versa Tool make it simple to adjust the amount of heat your pen emits. This makes it a perfect tool for working on numerous tasks simultaneously. It also offers a highly useful and ergonomic handle for prolonged usage with minimum strain.

The supplied heat protection protects your hand for more comfort

This wood-burning tool kit also has many features and is a preferred option for various projects like burning wood, shading, calligraphy, soldering, and more. The tips included are a universal point, a conical point, a floating point, a calligraphy point, a shading point, a transfer point, a soldering point, and hot knifepoint.

This is a great starter pyrography toolkit for anyone looking to get started with all of these features with less capital. Get this device if you are looking for the best wood tools at a great price!

CHAPTER THREE

PROJECT LIFE CYCLE

PREPARATORY CHECKS FOR WOODBURNING

Before you start working on a project, you should first become familiar with the tool. Take a piece of choice wood, insert the woodburning tool into an electrical socket, let it heat up for about 5 minutes, and try out the "design" on wood with various tips like you would with a pencil. It's an easy step. You may allow the tool to cool down for 5 minutes before changing bits. It should be reheated for a few minutes if the wood doesn't burn the way you want it. The key is to move forward slowly and steadily.

OTHER INDICATORS TO WATCH OUT FOR

It's a good practice to keep a wet towel close to wipe the top of the tip every time wood debris builds up. If you get too much smoke, the pen is too hot. Try lowering the heat for a softer, smoother burn. Pay attention to the safety guidelines. Always pay attention to the position of the hot metal tip. Make sure it doesn't touch anything and always rests on the metal base when not in use. Use pliers wrapped in electrical tape to change bits as the edges will stay hot for a long time.

SELECT A DESIGN

One of the most inspiring aspects of the art of the woodburning process is making a selection of a good design. The possibilities for anything you can turn into a piece of wood are endless. You can have access to endless varieties of images and designs from which to choose around you, the works of others, or from the internet. As a beginner, it's recommended that you go for a simple one. Simply type "pyrography images" in a search engine and you will find endless varieties to choose from.

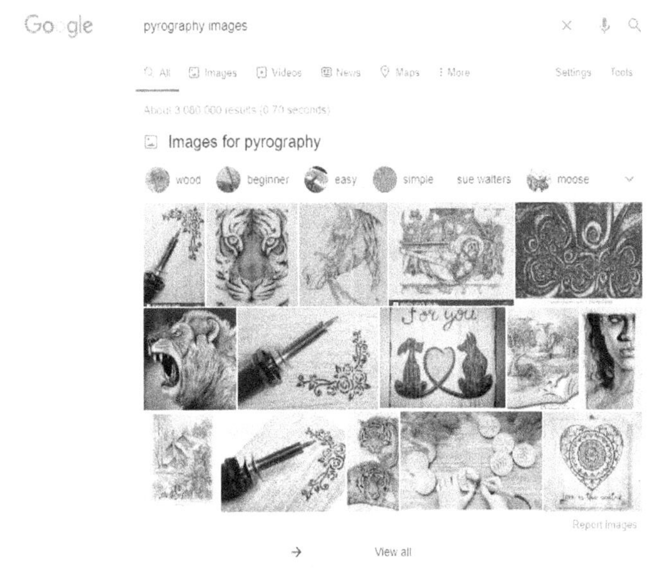

There can be no shortage of wood types to choose from. Softwoods burn at lower a temperature while hardwoods require a higher temperature. The next step is to sand the surface for smooth and easy-going tracing and burning. Be sure to identify the grain and burn in harmony with its direction as this will afford a smooth-running burn than going in the opposite direction. Also, keep the grain horizontal for a seamless process.

Additionally, you can use pre-made woodwork such as boxes or cut shapes that you can find at any hobby store. Anything you buy pre-made from a hobby store is very easy to work with and you don't have to be anxious about grain issues.

PLACING YOUR DESIGN ON WOOD

Glue your cut design (a wide frame is nice, as long as it fits on the board) onto carbon paper and then to the board. Tape the image you've cut out onto the carbon paper, and thereafter place it on the wood surface. Use a pencil to precisely outline your design.

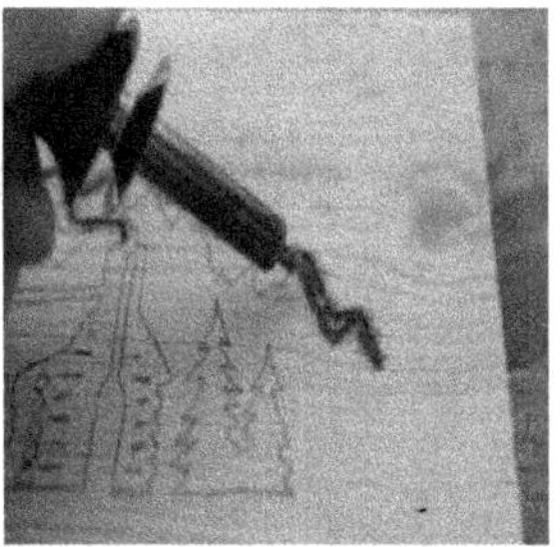

Place your design on the medium and

BURNING THE BORDERLINES

With your pen already heated, follow the carbon line found on the wooden surface and burn along the grain as much as possible. Remember that you are still fallible as a beginner. Practice makes less imperfection. So practice, practice, and practice, and you will be rewarded with beautiful crafts of your own making.

Tracing the outline with your pen

COLOR INTEGRATION AND FINISHING

Having completed the outline, the next step is shading. This involves adding color to the art. After burning, you may want to add color to your pyrography. You can do this with a variety of different art elements, such as watercolor pencils, crayons or waxed-based oil pencils, gel paints, or wooden gel stains.

Color integration makes your art more professional

COLORING TECHNIQUES

Depending on the kind of tip used, a vast array of colors and tones may be created. Depending on how the metal is placed on the material or the temperature, various effects are produced. Typically, wood is painted after the pattern has been burnt. The delicate grain of light hardwoods including beech and birch is used more often than that of figs. Other trees, like ash, maple, pine, and oak, are also used. Using the same heat-ironing procedure, pyrography is also employed on leather items. The skin is characterized by dramatic patterns and also allows for very subtle shading.

CHAPTER FOUR

PROJECT EXECUTION

PROJECT 1: MAKE A WOODEN CHEESE

Assuming you already own a wooden sign or choose to construct your own, you may adorn your table with fire-burning implements as needed. The process requires some tools and a short time. Be sure to prepare your work area as discussed earlier and get your materials ready.

BURN YOUR CHEESEBOARD TO WOOD

STEP 1

Draw your drawing on the board with a pencil. Once you've determined the design that you want to create on your dashboard, find out what other elements you may need to design the dashboard. Simple geometric shapes usually look better. Follow this path and use a ruler to perfect your pencil.

In addition to any recognizable suggestions or images, you'll need to create something more creative, such as B. a drawing on the edge of the boat or even a flock of geese flying on the surface of the boat.

Another great option: create a picture of a child created by you or one of your children. The board has special meaning for your family, but it can also have a smile on your face.

STEP 2

Use other devices to publish your design. For designs such as classic letters, arrows, or trees, you can purchase several instruments instead of hand-making the design. Ex, use a swipe to easily find a pattern on the dashboard. You can also use graphite paper to draw a more complex design directly on the wood.

You can find more templates and toner paper in art stores or online.

STEP 3

Warm up the wooden tool. Pick an edge, place it on the tool, and heat it. Ensure that the tool is switched on.

Many wooden tools have different tips. Based on your model, you can use a sharp edge (great for sewing) or a flat head with a screwdriver to create lines with a tip width at a time.

Wood-burning tools and more tips can be discovered on the internet or at most craft stores.

STEP 4

Follow the pencil lines. With the wood tool, press firmly against the pencil lines you drew on the board. You may have to cross the lines several times to get enough rust.

When you finish the firing step, let the wood cool and erase any missing pencil lines.

STEP 5

Paint the wood naturally. You can paint the wood before seasoning it for aesthetic reasons so that it is safe to use in food. If you want, make a natural stain by mixing highly concentrated coffee with balsamic vinegar. Paint the solution on the wood, let it dry, and let it look old.

To produce very concentrated coffee, grind the usual number of coffees for a batch, but add just a cup or two of hot water to the French press. Before straining the coffee, soak it in water, then combine it with the balsamic vinegar.

BOARD SEASONING AND MAINTENANCE

STEP 1

Choose spice oil. Before using the cheese for cutting and serving, you need to place a new or burnt cheese platter. This prevents plaque or bacterial odor and protects against bacteria and mold growth. For seasoning, the oil must first be applied, and then a new normal oil to keep the pores of the wood full.

Standard mineral oil in USP quality especially for the initial treatment of joints. In addition to being cheap, mineral oil is safe and does not wear out. Do not mix mineral oil with mineral spirits.

Mineral oil is sometimes called liquid paraffin and is available at pharmacies, online, or at your local hardware store. A glass of oil should be enough to fill your dashboard.

Avoid using most vegetable or edible oils, such as olive oil or canola, as they will deteriorate.

Walnut, almond, or coconut oils will slow down but eventually become brittle. Therefore, these lubricants are better suited to seasoning with cheese.

STEP 2

Spread the oil generously. Warm the oil used for sweetening before application. Soak the microwave in a glass of oil over high heat for 30 seconds. Dip a clean cloth in the oil and distribute it evenly on the wood. Leave the oil on the wood for a while. Six hours between coats, then wipe the remaining oil off the wood surface.

Repeat the procedure 4 or 5 times until the entire wood is wet.

Coat the instrument panel with a new coat of oil every month. Don't worry about too much oil. After about six hours, wipe off any oil that has not penetrated the wood.

STEP 3

The board is completed with a layer of beeswax. Beeswax may be incorporated into the oil used to season wood, or it can be used after seasoning to refine the wood. In any case, beeswax helps the wood to withstand water and protects it from normal wear and tear.

Mix the light with mineral oil for about a glass of mineral oil and half a teaspoon in the microwave over high heat for 45 seconds. Always use it while the mixture is still hot.

To apply a coating, wipe a clean cloth with the wax block until the wax is evenly covered with tar on the surface of the fabric. Rub the cloth on the cheeseboard and buff the level. Let the varnish dry before bending the wood to a long, fragrant sheen.

CHEESE CLEANING AND STORAGE

STEP 1

Clean your card after each use. Use warm soapy water to clean your table and clean it with a soft hairbrush or sponge. After washing, rinse with a clean cloth and dry.

To remove the lingering odor, apply coarse sea salt or baking soda to the wood and let it sit for a few minutes. Clean and rinse the material.

Rub a lemon wedge on your table surface to extract the special aroma of onions and garlic.

STEP 2

Avoid damaging your motherboard. Incorrect storage is the most likely way to ruin your cheese platter. To avoid this, put the card in a dry place and prop it up vertically without pressing on either side.

Never leave a wooden cheese tray submerged in water while cleaning the table.

Never use a wire brush or wire rope to clean the wooden cheese.

STEP 3

Disinfect your table regularly. There are several ways to disinfect the control panel. The most popular is cleaning the board with clear white vinegar. After each cleaning, sprinkle the plate with vinegar to disinfect it.

After wiping the dashboard with vinegar, wipe it with a paper towel dipped in 3% hydrogen peroxide, especially if you are concerned that bacteria will spread to your dashboard.

For a very strong disinfectant solution, mix liquid bleach with vinegar in a ratio of 1: 5. Leave this mixture on the plate for a few minutes, then rinse and pat dry.

CREATE/SELECT A WOOD CHEESEBOARD

STEP 1

Make a separate cheese board. You can cut the cheese you want to burn. To do this, you will need, among other things, a parquet, a puzzle, and a powerful grinder. First, pull the cheese from the tree without tying it to the tree.

After the gentle cutting, ideally, smooth all the edges with a jigsaw and rub the first with 80 pebbles and another 220 extra fine stones.

STEP 2

Buy a regular cheese board. Maybe it is a good idea to buy a simple cheese board and wood with the design you want. One factor to consider is the size and weight of your card. When making decisions consider things like the most common uses of field and fusion. You can find cheese on the internet and in kitchen stores.

STEP 3

Choose a wooden board that you like. Another factor to consider when adding your design, especially to a wood-burning stove, is the wood design. Natural leaves also have a natural vein that can often be seen on the leaf surface.

Some of the cheese produced shows the last grain of the forest. These are also great if you have a lot of time to spend on your dashboard. Regardless of the method of construction, you need to pay attention to the design of the carpenter, without the design that you want to add to yourself.

PROJECT 2: HOW TO MAKE A WOODEN LETTER

A great way to add a decorative touch to any wood surface is to burn letters on wood. It's also a great way to bookmark an item so users know it is yours. If you want to carve wooden letters, prepare your surface, find the right tools, and prepare your design. After making these preparations, you can use your wood-burning stove to write the message you want on the tree.

SURFACE PREPARATION

STEP 1

Choose wood. Every wooden surface can burn. However, some are better than others. Light, a softwood-like perch works particularly well. This is because the firewood stands out in its bright color and you don't have to push too much to leave a mark.

Less-grained trees are also better suited for burning wood. Woodgrain can make firewood lines uneven and inaccurate. With less-grained wood, you can draw smoother, more precise lines

STEP 2

Prepare the wood surface. If you're burning wood, you'll want to start with a smooth, polished surface. While it is possible to burn wood on a rough surface, it is easier to burn wood on a smooth surface and the result is always cleaner.

STEP 3

Apply the coatings to the surface in such a way that the wood burns. Burning paint or stains can produce very toxic fumes that are not good to breathe.

STEP 4

Use a stencil or freely draw letters on the board. The easiest way to put your drawing on your tree is to draw it directly with a pencil. This can be done freely or with stencils or stencils for a more accurate design.

You can also edit your letters hands-free with the oven. However, once you start burning wood it will be easier to follow a pattern in the wood.

STEP 5

Transfer your design to the wood. Create a design on paper or a computer and transfer it to your wooden surface. First, draw the design on a piece of paper or create it on a computer and then print it out. Then place a piece of carbon paper on the board and place the drawing paper on top of the carbon paper. When you find your drawing, take a pencil or pencil and transfer it onto the wooden surface.

STEP 6

When applying carbonated paper to your wood, make sure the carbon side of the paper is facing the wood. The top is usually shiny in comparison.

STEP 7

Use one end of the image transfer cooker. There is a technique that you can use to transfer photocopied images onto wood using your wooden plank. Purchase an image transfer tip for the iron sold specifically for this technique. Spread the paper on the board. Then gradually warm the back of the paper with the image transfer edge. The heat from the iron drives the ink away from the photocopy and onto the surface of the wood.

This process can only be done by photocopying. This procedure won't work if you have an inkjet printer.

To do this, use a special tip for your wooden board. If your iron doesn't have any of these tips, contact the manufacturer to check availability.

TOOLS PREPARATION

- **Get an iron:** There is a wide selection of wood panels in craft and hobby stores, as well as online stores. Wood stoves are often accompanied by elbows, heat management, and various ends. If you are new to wood-burning stoves, you can buy a base model to see if you like firewood without spending a lot of money. The price of wood panels can vary significantly depending on the amount of heat and the type of heat control involved. You need to find a simple wood stove for around $ 40. However, high-quality stoves used by professionals can cost over $ 200.

- **Choose a tip:** Most wooden irons have a set of ends that screw into the end of the burner. Tips are usually available in a variety of sizes. Usually, when you want to complete a detailed task, use a short sentence. Choose a bigger tip to make the letters bigger and thicker. In addition to large and small edges, different edge shapes create different types of lines. For example, the crown of your tree could break. This is done for the shadow. There are also tips for drawing straight lines that are wedge-shaped and reach a point on the page. While the iron is hot, replace the tip with a pair of pliers. Pliers protect your hands from hot iron.

- **Use special tips:** Some ovens have special tips that are basic brands. They are shaped iron edges on the surface that can burn the wood with a simple drilling operation. In some cases these special tips contain text. Once you have the writing tips for your project, you can write on the board clearly and quickly. If you use special stamp tips, change the tips for each letter individually. Be careful and remember to use pliers as the edges will get very hot.

- **Heat your iron:** Tie it tight and let it warm up for a few minutes. The instructions that came with the iron will give you an idea of how long your iron will take to heat up. Allow the iron to warm up before use so that the combustion lines are stable and well-defined. If your iron has temperature control, make sure it is set to the temperature you want. If you want to create straight lines, you usually need an iron with a temperature of 371 ° C. If you want to shade something, set your iron to a softer temperature.

USE A WOOD-BURNING TOOL
FIRST STAGE

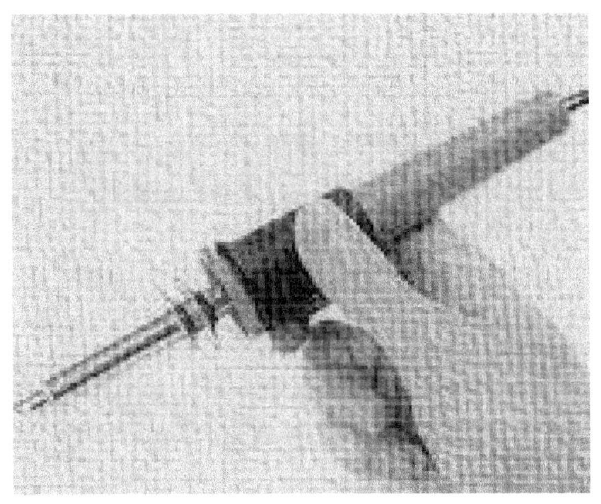

Hold the burner firmly, but gently press the wood together. Keep it in place while burning so the wood doesn't slip out of your hands and burn. However, it is not necessary to press the wood too hard. A properly heated board should be able to easily burn medium-strength wood.

However, you can play around with the pressure you put on the surface to have different effects on wood burning. For example, if you want a darker area in your design and press harder, the burns will get deeper and darker.

SECOND STAGE

Always move on the surface of the wood. When you start to burn, use a constant speed to keep your lines even. As you change your speed, some areas of your lines will become thicker than others. Because the slower it goes, the more wood the iron has to burn.

It may take some practice to get a stable network. If clean lines are your thing, take some time to stitch your technique onto a piece of wood before burning the wood in your project.

THIRD STAGE

Follow the letters. Start the tracking process by finding your mailing list. Use gentle motions and don't stop the moving center lines. For smooth, even lines, your lines only start and end at the end of the lines in your letters.

For example, the letter O should be written on a single line. The letter R can be written on three lines: vertical line, upper arch, and foot in the lower right corner.

FOURTH STAGE

Adjust the temperature of your iron. If you find that your stripes are too light or too dark, you may need to change the temperature of your iron. The temperature you need depends on your technique and the type of wood used. Hence, you may need to tweak it a bit to get the results you want.

If you have an iron without temperature control, the temperature will be less regulated. If this type of iron doesn't get hot enough after a few strokes, wait for the iron to warm up before continuing.

FIFTH STAGE

Fill in the letters. If your design is in bold you may need to go back and fill it in after the letter is in the center. Just use the same light pressure and movement as the contours.

If you want to fill large areas, don't use a small tip. Using a small pen to complete a large area takes a long time and can cause color differences.

SIXTH STAGE

Add extra details to your design. After you've written the letters on the chalkboard, it's time to add additional decorations like decorative folds or small flowers.

PROJECT 3: MAKING VARIOUS DECORATIONS

In addition to the marker, you will also need pieces of wood. If you plan to make this yourself, you will need dry wood, a saw, a drill, and some sandpaper. Pen, Watercolor, snow decoration, or white glitter for kids (optional), and Elbow thread.

HOW TO MAKE A HOUSE SIGNAL

STAGE 1

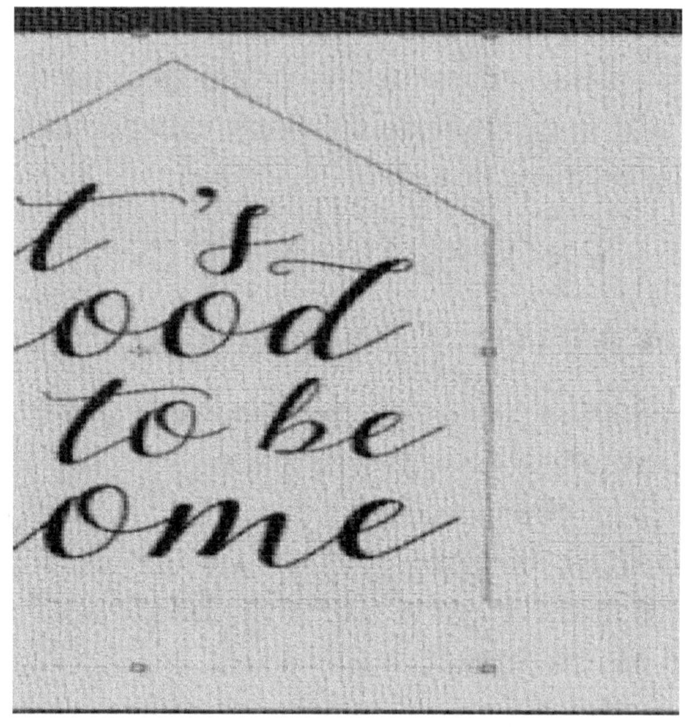

Measure the plate: When creating a design, leave 5mm around the edge to make sure it fits. The font that appears is the velvet flower. You can find the free fonts available with a quick internet search. After you've created your design, use the design software's settings to flip the image horizontally and print it on tracing paper.

STAGE 2

Cut off any excess tracing paper and drop and hold the ink on the plate.

STAGE 3

Use the embossing tool to gently rub the image to transfer the ink to the plate. Peel off the paper towel.

STAGE 4

The pyrograph should be heated for about five to ten minutes. Use a rounded edge as it will flow more easily when burned.

HOW TO CREATE A HEART SIGN

STAGE 1

Trace around the heart on plain paper. This allows you to draw designs knowing they will fit on the plate.

STAGE 2

When you receive your drawing, copy it onto the board with a pencil.

STAGE 3

The pyrography tool should be heated for about five to ten minutes.

STAGE 4

Use a rubber band to remove pencil marks after baking.

HOW TO BURN WOODEN EARRINGS

Required materials:

➤ Plaid 2-in-1 Woodburning Craft Tool

- ➢ Wood branded decorations
- ➢ Washi tape
- ➢ Martha Stewart Crafts Multi-Surface Satin. Paint in different colors
- ➢ Martha Stewart Crafts Gold Liquid Glitter
- ➢ Paint Brushes
- ➢ Jump rings
- ➢ Fishhook earring findings
- ➢ Jewelry pliers

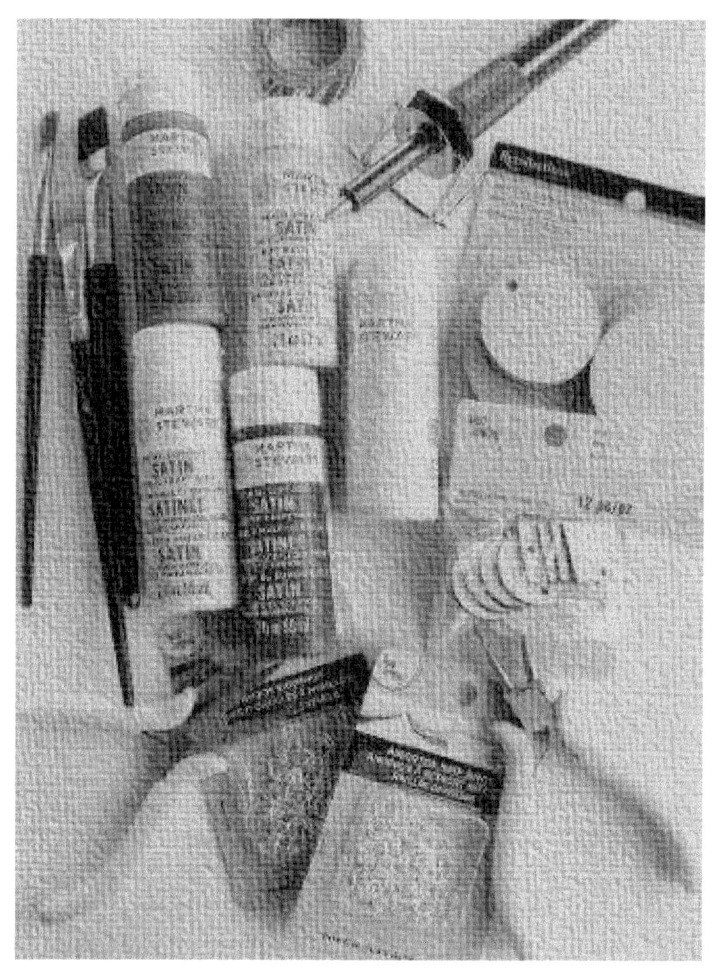

Equip the wood tool with the chisel tip. Connect and activate the vehicle. Let it warm up completely.

As the tool heats up, use the tip to carefully create patterns on the wood. Some fun options are honeycombs like the following, which are created by placing the flat end of the tool on the surface of the wooden circle to create six adjacent hexagonal edges.

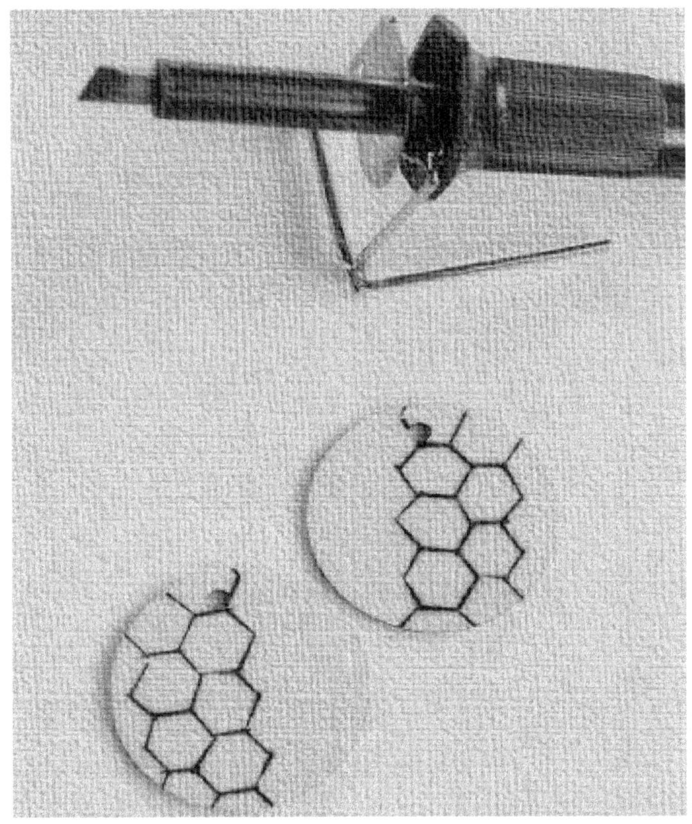

But you can't go wrong playing and experimenting to create a design that suits your imagination. If you're using a wood-burning tool, I love the point of the chisel as it helps create precise, straight lines for geometric shapes like hexagons, triangles, and squares. TIP: When decorating the discs, try

making a mirror so that the earrings have a
balanced design when you wear them.

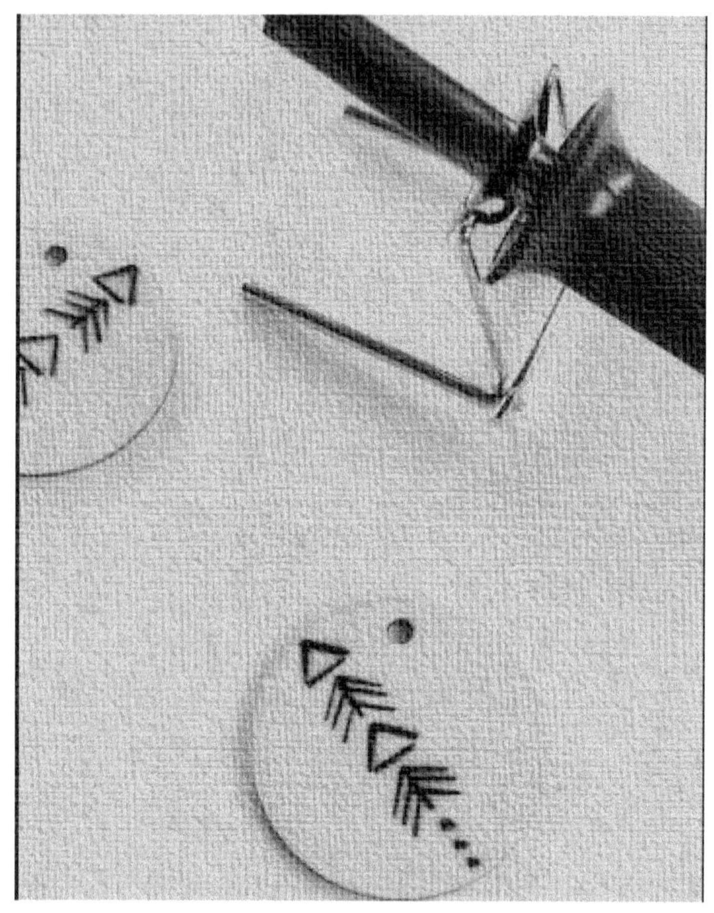

When the fired pattern is done, cover the
pattern with washi tape and then use a brush
to apply the paint and/or liquid to both sides
of the gold-plated part, applying the paint
away from the tape with brush strokes. The
bleeding stain from below let the paint dry for

15 minutes before removing the tape and setting the shapes aside.

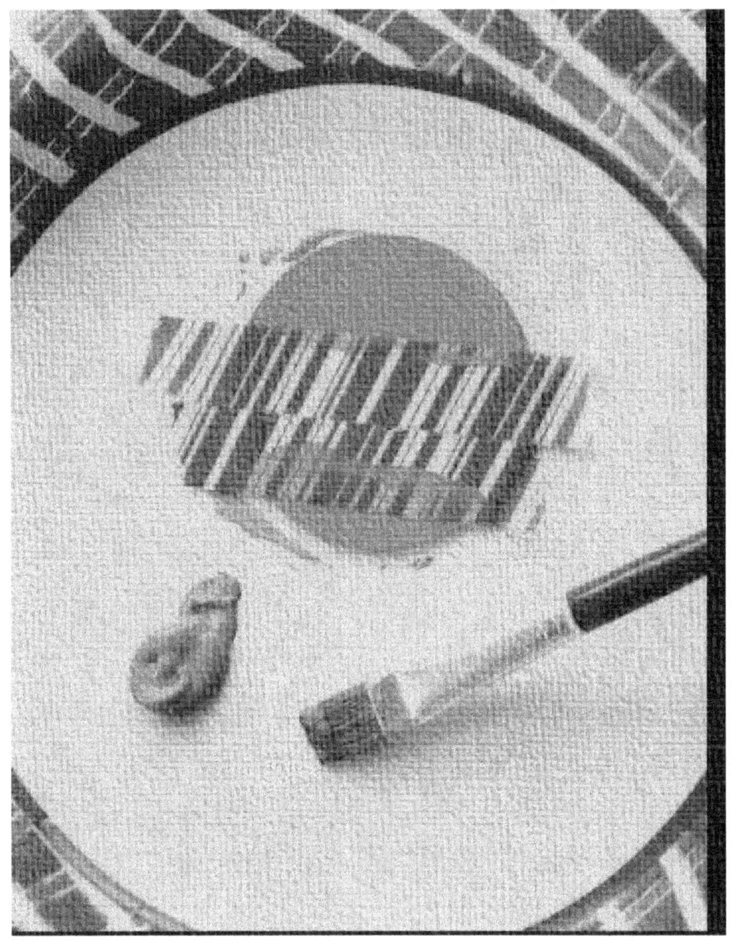

Use pliers to attach a 1/8-inch jump ring to the loop on the bottom of each ear detector.

Use pliers to create a larger spring ring (the size required will depend on the size of the wooden circle you are using, but mine is 1/4 for reference), then thread the ring through the top hole. Disc.

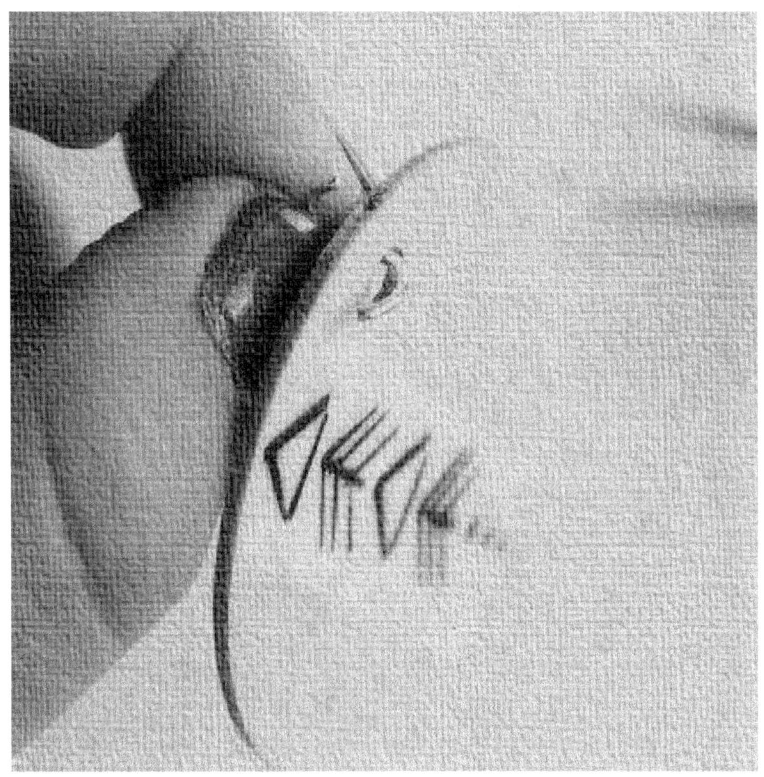

Insert the small spring into the larger spring ring, making sure that the hook is pointing in the right direction when you carry it.

Close the large spring with pliers to secure everything in place. Repeat these steps to repair other found objects for the remaining wooden tray.

The use of different sizes and shapes of wooden shapes, as well as different colors and designs, make this a great gift idea that can be customized to suit each buyer's style!

CHAPTER FIVE

SAFETY CONSIDERATIONS

As the saying goes, "there is a pain in beauty", it is important to note that pyrography is flirting with fire. At the end of your work come elegant designs greatly admired, but it does not come without risks. Therefore, safety measures and rules need to be observed.

In this chapter, we will discuss the basic and advanced measures that you need to know as a beginner and as well as a professional Woodburner.

BASIC SAFETY GUIDELINES

1. Do not touch the metal when the machine is on: Many have suffered unnecessary injuries for not following this simple rule of common sense. One reason some people do this is that sometimes it's hard to tell if the point burner is on or hot enough to burn. So if you want to see if it's hot the natural reaction is to lightly touch it. Move your hand over two inches of the metal to feel if heat is coming from the metal. Better yet, place the tip on a piece of wood for a few seconds to see if it starts to burn.

If you're struggling to keep those itchy fingers from pushing their limits, then resort to a pair of gloves or finger guards.

2. Keep your burner away from flammable materials:

It's easy to clutter your work surface or accidentally set paper pyrography patterns or burn patterns too close to your burning tool or melt things that you don't understand are too close. Stay away from this hot machine.

3. Secure the loose suspension: Things like hair, jewelry, and headphones

4. Work on a hard and durable surface such as a table or desk: Your work surface should be wider than your workpiece and need to be stable on a level surface. This prevents you from burning your leg or boring a hole in your couch.

5. Attach the base to the table: Fixed points. Wire tip base. Do not pierce the carpet.

Usually, you don't have to worry about cable torches. But fixed burners usually have a light metal base that fits loosely on your table. When you place your tool on the base, the base will slide off the table due to the weight of the pen. Tape it. Attach it to a larger piece of wood that looks like a weight.

6. Always place the pen on the base when you are not using it:

If you don't, you will regret it. Hit the rope once and those lovely pants you wear will have a new breathing hole for your knee.

7. Turn off your burner while leaving the table:

It's as dangerous as leaving the oven when you're not home. Don't let it cook alone, wastes electricity and maybe burns the house. Shut it down. If you need to leave the room, unplug it to take extra precautions.

8. Use metal tongs to remove the pyrography tips or attach them to a hot burner:

For wire torches with interchangeable tips, tweezers are usually made for this purpose. Simply turn off the machine, gently pull the tip, and place the tip in a heat-resistant container. Screwing wire tips on pyrography tips do not require pliers or tweezers as you use a screwdriver to insert or remove the tips. Pliers are for fixed-point burners. Do this carefully. Warm ends bend easily. Carefully remove the tip from the burner tube. Then put your tip in a heat-resistant container. First, insert the new air tip by hand and use a pair of pliers to gently but quickly tighten the tip.

Note: When the burner starts to boil, the cold ends will heat up quickly. If the torch is hot when you change bits, your cold tip will heat up in seconds and become too hot to reinstall by hand. If necessary, use pliers or a pair of leather gloves to reattach the tip.

9. Favor using dry, non-toxic, untreated wood for your burning medium: If you burn something other than wood - cloth, bones, cork, etc., make sure these things are free of chemicals, processes, adhesives, stains, and surfaces.

10. Teach children the safety of burning tools. Keep hot tools out of their reach:

The inexperienced people are not aware of the risks associated with their job.

Pyrography can be a very fun hobby, but there are a few risk factors to be aware of. Concerns have been raised regarding the safety of the art, particularly when it comes to breathing in smoke from burning wood. Although this is an apparent issue, there are additional things you should be aware of before you begin burning wood. In addition to gases, there is an extremely real risk of fire and sawdust that may be breathed or cause skin irritation.

OTHER SAFETY CONCERNS
(FOR PROFESSIONALS)

TOXIC FUMES INHALED DURING THE BURNING PROCESS

The reality is that a variety of factors influence the toxicity of this smoke. It is thus prudent to err on the side of caution. You ought to study and consult an expert on the hazards of any new wood and the species you want to use. Despite the fact that certain gases are less harmful than others, each form has inherent dangers.

Before beginning a wood-burning project, you must consider the following. Regardless of whether there is no way to eliminate it entirely, you must make every effort to reduce the hazards. Leave a few fans running and the open the windows to guarantee sufficient ventilation. This will prevent smoke from entering the atmosphere and your lungs. Choose timbers that are reasonably non-toxic. With so many accessible solutions, there is no need to put your health at danger.

WOOD TYPE YOU SHOULD NOT USE

Painted, stained, pressure applied, sculpted, etc. It is essential to prevent using certain woods. Even after extensive sanding or cleaning, the chemicals from these operations may remain deeply embedded in the wood and continue to combust it. It may be quite dangerous to your health. Avoid dealing with synthetic or modified wood wherever possible. Also, to be avoided are plywood and Medium-Density Fibreboard. They have been modified by man and contain formaldehyde; for that reason, we want to refrain from using them. Some artists opt to work with plywood, however burning the wood layer and melting the adhesive may be hazardous to health. So, we avoid it completely.

There's a little more value in buying good, freshly cut wood and avoiding these undesirable health risk factors. You may want to get rid of man-made chemicals from your fresh wood whenever and wherever possible.

WOOD IDENTIFICATION

Before you begin, it is important to identify and study what types of wood you are burning. Each wood has its unique properties and levels of toxicity. You may be affected by smoke from some kind of wood substance, but farewell with others. Besides, consider those around you as well. Think about the effect of smoke or sawdust on the health of anyone that may enter your work area and may be exposed to it.

EXPOSURE TO SAWDUST DURING PYROGRAPHY

Despite the fact that smoke is the primary concern for many individuals, you need to be cautious of the sawdust it generates. The dust produced by sanding wood poses a danger of inhalation into the nose, mouth, throat, and lungs. Adding to the essence that is discharged into the canvas, it may also cause skin irritation. Whenever feasible, you should sand your components outside to prevent this issue. This will prevent dust from getting caught in your work area and causing breathing issues. Some artists prefer to use gloves when working with wood as some types can irritate your skin.

Again, this should be discussed with an expert before choosing a type of tree to work with. Only a specialist can give you accurate information about all health risks of a particular type.

WHAT TO DO IF YOU HAVE HEALTH PROBLEMS

Stop working immediately if you have health difficulties. When you're working and experience difficulty in breathing, or a burning sensation in your eyes, skin, or throat, consult a health expert immediately. Smoke, dust, or essence may cause a reaction.

TALK TO AN EXPERT:

We're confident that you will conduct your research on the wood you're working with, including advice from an expert. It is a good idea to ask about the harmful effects that could be caused by burning, using, cutting, or grinding a particular machine.

CHAPTER SIX

TIPS FOR PROFESSIONAL WOODBURNING

CONSIDER BUYING A TIP/PEN WOOD-BURNING SYSTEM.

If you want to change bits frequently, it can be a time saver. Pyrography burners can reach temperatures between 400 and 565 degrees Celsius. Solid screw burners often use soft brass. It may take five minutes or more for the tip of this metal to cool to a temperature that you can safely remove with your fingers. You can shorten this time with pliers, but it is not recommended because you can easily remove the threads of this soft metal if you try to remove the tip while it is still hot.

However, for cable torches with a nose and pencil combo, you can replace the entire handle even if the edges are hot. You don't have to wait for the tip to cool. This can be very easy when you need to use different tips in a project.

NOTE THAT SMALLER GAUGE TIPS USUALLY TAKE LONGER TO WARM UP.

The following rule of thumb applies to cable meters: the smaller the meter number, the thicker the wire. You should note that pyrography instruments take longer to heat a thick wire. For example, a 16-gauge tip takes longer to warm up than a 20-gauge tip.

IDENTIFY THE FOLLOWING TIPS AND USES FOR THESE CABLE BURN TIPS:

Here are some general tips for burning "wire end" wood:

- The hollow end has an angled or curved comb tip. Most people often use this tip for long lines like burning big hair.

- The spearhead has a sharp point. Many people use this tip to get into tight spaces and burn fine details.
- The rounded Edge has a circular tip. This advice is desirable when depression is undesirable.
- The tip of the chisel has a point that shines perpendicular to the side edges. Many people use this tip to train their backlines.
- The ballpoint pen tip has a small ball glued to the top of the tip. Many people use this tip when a natural writing gesture is desired.

THE FOLLOWING "HARD POINT" SHOULD BE ABLE TO IDENTIFY WOOD BURN TIPS AND THEIR BEST USE.

Some common tips for burning solid wood:

i. Many people use the general (general) tip to lighten the outline of patterns and create straight lines.

ii. The calligraphy nib is great for curved lines and natural writing.

iii. The ultra-fine tip is often used for detailed work to create straight lines and narrow curves.

iv. Many people use the shading tip to fill and shade large areas and add shadows.

1. Note that softer, lower-density woods like linden burn faster and require less heat than the harder, denser ones.

Basswood is another popular wood since it has relatively fewer grains and the burning process produces a strong contrast between both the original wood and the burn's dark hue. Hardwoods such as maple, ash, and oak often demand more heat and burn at a slower rate.

2. Avoid contour marking when shading an area filled with a gradient.

Work over medium heat with circular movements. This will slowly darken an area. Gradient fill is harder to burn than black fill. It takes less warmth and more patience.

3. Follow the order used by most wood burners.

Most burners first prepare the wood chips for a smooth surface. Then, they transfer or draw a pattern on wood, possibly with carbon paper, graphite paper, or a soft pencil. Then light the contours and finally add fill and shading.

4. Keep in mind that you need to trace the outline of the design by burning it first.

By burning the contours, the wood is demarcated allowing you to focus on the piece you want to use for your work. Now you can apply stains to the area without worrying about staining the rest.

5. If possible, burn with the grain to make it easier.

As we have mentioned earlier, burning in the direction of the grain pays. It makes it easier to deal with than to work against the grain. Burning against grains generally offers more resistance.

6. Avoid subjecting the workpiece to intense pressure with the tip of your burning tool.

Contrary to what most beginners think, it doesn't take a lot of pressure to successfully burn wood. The slight pressure allows you to carefully guide the pen to get cute touches.

Light pressure also causes fewer errors and fewer accidental burns. Let the focal tips do the job instead of forcing. Also, be aware that excessive pressure can bend hot ends.

7. Avoid smoke when burning wood.

Wood combustion may emit toxic gases that pose major health risks. So, it is recommended that you do not work in a confined space. Instead, work in a well-ventilated area to avoid fumes inhalation. If you are working in an unventilated area, a smoke vent device similar to the GourdMaster Woodburning Buddy II is recommended.

8. If you want to change direction slightly, use a round, lighted wooden edge when burning.

The rounded edges or sphere's edges will not penetrate the wood as deeply as other kinds of edges. This provides you more mobility and facilitates easy direction changes. These characteristics make these tips ideal for writing and signing. However, chisels, wedge points, and spear points are more difficult to deflect.

9. Avoid pressurized wood, fiber medium density (MDF), and wood that is stained or stained when burned.

The chemical preservatives in pressure-treated wood protect it against termites, fungal decay, and insects. MDF panels can contain hazardous compounds including formaldehyde. Finally, stains and varnishes also contain chemicals that can produce harmful fumes when burned. However, most experts believe that the outer layer of plywood is safe for burning wood. Plywood is made up of three or more thin layers of wood that are glued together with glue. If you only burn the outer layers of plywood (with no glue), wood is a safe fuel.

10. Note that most 110-volt electrical markings take 15 to 20 minutes to reach operating temperature.

As soon as this temperature is reached, the marking iron can leave a good, dark impression on the wood in about 2-4 seconds. Marking irons without electricity (usually heated with a propane lens) can reach operating temperature in 2-3 minutes. In contrast to electric marking irons, non-electric marking irons need to be reheated between dimensions.

11. Understand that the area must be dead for a marker to work.

While it will make an impression at the bottom of a bowl, a smaller design will generally work best. Many carpenters, rather of building a "perfectly level" foundation, create a flat region beneath the plinth border in the middle of the base. This lower point ensures that the piece only sits on the edge and stands without vibration, even if the wood moves slightly over time.

CHAPTER SEVEN

PYROGRAPHY GALLERY INSPIRES

The look and feel of your work in the profession of pyrography depend, to a large extent, on the motivation you have. Fundamental to this is viewing the works of other professional wood-burning artists. This requires being an inquisitive person. Do not just look away when you observe a good finishing hung as a decoration in the home of a friend. Take a closer look. Leverage the power of imagination −think of the type of pyrography medium used, the system employed, and the artist's preferences and love of nature enshrined in that piece of artistic culture.

Pursuing pyrography as a career can be rewarding. But remember that it all starts with observation, admiration, and determination to achieve the fit that, at first, seems impossible. However, take the challenge and embark on your first project.

Below are some interesting works that will fill you with a sense of gratitude for the designers.

Leather
Pyrography

INDEX